AROHA TERESA

Lost Realm

Dedicated to God

Contents

Preface

In a world where magic and mystery intertwine, Emily Carter, a determined and resourceful young scholar, stumbles upon an ancient book that reveals the existence of a hidden realm. This realm, known as the Lost Realm, is on the brink of collapse, its delicate balance disrupted by dark forces and forgotten powers.

Emily's quest begins in the enigmatic Labyrinth of Echoes, where she uncovers the first clues to the realm's plight. Guided by cryptic messages and magical artifacts, she navigates through perilous trials and mystical landscapes, each step drawing her deeper into a web of ancient secrets.

As she ventures through the Enchanted Forest, battles the Firestorm Citadel, and confronts the perils of the Veiled Summit, Emily discovers the powerful Heart of the Realm, a crystal with the ability to restore balance. Yet, even with the Heart secured, the realm's troubles are far from over. The Awakening Storm, a chaotic force unleashed by the convergence of magical energies, threatens to undo all her hard-won progress.

In a final, intense confrontation, Emily must locate and stabilize the Tempest Stone at the Stormspire to quell the storm and secure the realm's future. Along the way, she learns that her journey is not just about saving a mystical land but also about understanding her own strength and the true nature of harmony and balance.

"Lost Realm" is a captivating tale of bravery, magic, and the enduring quest for equilibrium. Through Emily's journey, readers are taken on an epic adventure filled with rich, fantastical elements and profound discoveries about the power of unity and resilience.

Acknowledgement

Thanks for your support

1

The Vanishing Mist

Emily Carter had always loved the early mornings in her small, sleepy town. The air was crisp, the streets quiet, and the promise of a new day felt as fresh as the dew on the grass. But today, something was different. As she walked to her usual spot at the end of Maple Street, a thick, swirling mist had descended, blanketing the town in a ghostly veil.

The mist wasn't normal. It had crept in overnight, obscuring familiar landmarks and muting the usual morning sounds. Emily squinted through the dense fog, trying to make out the houses and shops that were usually visible from her porch. The normally vivid colors of her surroundings were muted, reduced to shades of gray and white. It was as if the world had been drained of its vibrancy.

As Emily walked further, the fog grew denser. She could barely see a few feet ahead of her. The mist seemed almost alive, moving in subtle, unpredictable patterns, swirling around her like an ethereal dance. She shivered, though not from the cold. There was something unnervingly eerie about the mist's behavior, something that sent a chill down her spine.

Emily reached the end of Maple Street, where the fog seemed to be even thicker. The town square, usually bustling with the early morning activity of shopkeepers setting up, was eerily silent. She could see the vague outlines of the buildings through the fog, but the details were obscured. Her favorite café, which was usually a warm and welcoming sight, was now a shadowy silhouette.

Determined to uncover the source of this strange phenomenon, Emily pressed on toward the square. As she walked, her footsteps echoed strangely in the mist, their sound muffled and distant. She noticed that the usual morning birds were silent, and the wind seemed to have vanished entirely. It was as if the entire world was holding its breath.

In the center of the square stood an old, ornate fountain, its water now hidden beneath a thick layer of mist. Emily approached it, noticing how the fog seemed to coil and swirl around the fountain's base. She reached out to touch the cool, damp stone, and as her fingers made contact, she felt a shiver, not just from the cold but from something deeper, a sensation that made her skin prickle.

Suddenly, the mist seemed to part just enough for her to see a figure standing across the square. The figure was cloaked in darkness, almost blending into the fog itself. Emily's heart raced as she tried to make out any distinguishing features, but the figure remained indistinct, a mere shadow in the shifting mist.

Before she could react, the figure began to move, drifting slowly toward her. Emily's instinct was to run, but her feet felt rooted to the ground. The figure's movement was eerily graceful, as if it was gliding rather than walking. Emily's breath came in quick, shallow bursts as the figure drew nearer, the mist swirling around it in a mesmerizing dance.

When the figure was only a few feet away, it stopped and seemed to dissolve into the fog, leaving behind only a faint, lingering chill. Emily stood there, frozen, trying to make sense of what she had just seen. Her mind raced with questions and possibilities, none of which seemed to offer any comfort.

The fog began to lift slightly, revealing more of the town square. Emily saw that the mist had left a residue on the cobblestones, a strange, silvery sheen that glistened in the weak morning light. She bent down to examine it, but as she touched the residue, it evaporated into thin air, leaving no trace of its presence.

Feeling a mix of fear and determination, Emily straightened up and took a deep breath. She knew that the mist was not just an ordinary weather phenomenon. Something was profoundly wrong, and she needed to find out what.

As she turned to head back home, her mind was already racing with theories and possibilities. The town's old stories about mysterious happenings and hidden realms flashed through her thoughts. Perhaps there was more to the mist than met the eye. Emily resolved to uncover the truth, no matter where it might lead.

The mist continued to swirl around her, and as Emily walked away from the town square, she couldn't shake the feeling that this was just the beginning of something far greater, and far more dangerous, than she could ever have imagined.

2

Echoes of the Past

Emily Carter awoke to another gray morning, the mist from the previous day still clinging to the edges of her world like a persistent memory. She rubbed her eyes, trying to shake off the remnants of a restless night filled with unsettling dreams about shadowy figures and cryptic whispers. Her breakfast was a hurried affair; the fog outside had not lifted, and the familiar routine of her small town seemed strangely alien.

Determined to find answers, Emily decided to visit the town library. It was an old building with creaky wooden floors and dusty shelves, filled with the accumulated knowledge and history of her town. Her grandfather had always told her that the library was a treasure trove of stories, both real and imagined. Now, she hoped it might hold some clues about the mist that had descended on the town.

The bell above the library door jingled softly as Emily entered.

The librarian, Mrs. Hargrove, looked up from her desk, her expression one of mild surprise at the early visitor. Her hair was pulled back into a tight bun, and her glasses rested on the tip of her nose.

"Good morning, Emily. What brings you here so early?" Mrs. Hargrove asked, her voice a soothing balm against the tension Emily felt.

"I need to look up some old records," Emily replied, trying to keep her voice steady. "Something strange happened yesterday, and I'm hoping to find out if there's any history to explain it."

Mrs. Hargrove's eyes narrowed thoughtfully. "Well, you might be interested in the archives section. It's filled with old newspapers and historical documents. I'll get the key for you."

Emily thanked her and made her way to the back of the library. The archives room was dimly lit, with rows of old filing cabinets and shelves lined with dusty volumes. Emily's heart raced with anticipation as she began to sift through the records, searching for anything related to the mysterious mist.

She started with the newspapers. The crinkling of the old paper seemed louder in the quiet room. She scanned headlines and articles, looking for any mention of strange weather phenomena or unusual events. Hours passed, and her search seemed fruitless until she stumbled upon an article dated from over fifty years ago. The headline read: "Mysterious Fog Envelopes Town: No Explanation Found."

Emily's pulse quickened as she read the article. It described a similar fog that had covered the town, causing widespread confusion and concern. The article mentioned that local authorities had been baffled by the phenomenon, and it had eventually dissipated without any explanation. There were no further follow-ups or clarifications, leaving the incident shrouded in mystery.

She found another article in a different newspaper from the same time period. This one focused on local legends and folklore. It spoke of a long-forgotten tale about a hidden realm that lay beyond the town, accessible only through mysterious mists that appeared once in a great while. The legend suggested that those who ventured into the mist were drawn into a parallel world, where ancient powers and forgotten beings dwelled.

Emily's thoughts raced. Could the fog she had seen be connected to this lost realm? The idea seemed far-fetched, yet the similarity between the descriptions was too striking to ignore. She decided to dig deeper into the library's collection of local history books and records.

As the day wore on, Emily discovered more references to the hidden realm and the mysterious fog. She found old maps showing regions around the town marked with cryptic symbols and vague warnings. It became clear that there was a pattern of strange occurrences linked to these mists, suggesting that they had appeared throughout history under similar circumstances.

Exhausted but determined, Emily left the library as the sun began to set, casting long shadows over the fog-covered streets.

The library's front door creaked shut behind her, and she took a deep breath, the cool air filled with the same mist that had plagued her the day before.

Walking home, Emily felt a growing sense of urgency. The fog was not just a natural phenomenon but seemed to be a gateway or a sign of something much more significant. The echoes of the past were calling to her, urging her to explore further and uncover the truth behind the legend.

As she reached her house, Emily glanced back at the town, shrouded in the misty veil. She knew that her investigation was just beginning. The pieces of the puzzle were slowly falling into place, but there were still many unanswered questions. What was the hidden realm? Why did the mist appear now? And what did it mean for her and her town?

With a mixture of anticipation and trepidation, Emily resolved to continue her search. The echoes of the past had stirred something within her, and she was determined to follow them wherever they might lead, even if it meant venturing into the unknown depths of the Lost Realm.

3

The Hidden Portal

The fog had settled over the town with an eerie persistence, casting an otherworldly pallor over familiar streets and buildings. Emily Carter had spent the previous day at the library, piecing together fragments of history that hinted at a hidden realm. The ancient records and local legends painted a picture of a mystical place shrouded in secrecy, accessible only through rare and enigmatic mists. Now, as she stepped out of her house on the third morning of the fog's relentless grip, she felt a sense of urgency. She needed to explore further, to uncover the truth behind the strange occurrences.

The fog was denser than ever, swirling in heavy, almost tangible clouds that seemed to have a life of their own. Emily wrapped her coat tightly around herself, her breath forming small, ghostly puffs in the chilly air. She made her way to the edge of town, toward the area where the old records had mentioned an "ancient gateway" hidden in the woods.

The path leading into the forest was barely visible through the thick fog. Emily hesitated for a moment, the woods looking more foreboding than usual under the shroud of mist. Yet, she steeled herself and stepped onto the narrow trail, her footsteps crunching softly on the damp leaves.

The forest was silent, the usual rustle of wildlife strangely absent. The mist seemed to thicken the deeper she went, making it difficult to see more than a few feet ahead. Emily's senses were heightened, every sound amplified in the stillness. As she walked, she kept her eyes peeled for anything that might resemble a portal or gateway as described in the old texts.

After what felt like hours, she reached a small clearing. At its center stood an ancient stone archway, half-hidden by vines and overgrown vegetation. The arch was covered in moss and seemed almost to blend into the surroundings. Emily's heart skipped a beat. This was it—the gateway she had read about.

The archway was adorned with strange carvings, their significance lost to time. The symbols were intricate, winding in patterns that suggested both an ancient language and a deeper, hidden meaning. Emily traced the carvings with her fingers, feeling the cool stone beneath her touch. The symbols seemed to pulse faintly, and a low hum resonated through the archway.

Feeling a mix of awe and trepidation, Emily stepped through the arch. The moment she did, the mist around her seemed to swirl with renewed energy. She felt a sudden jolt, as if she had crossed an invisible threshold. The world around her shifted and shimmered.

On the other side, the forest appeared different. The trees were taller, their leaves an array of vibrant colors not seen in her world. The air was warmer, filled with a sweet, unfamiliar fragrance. The mist had cleared, revealing a landscape that was both beautiful and alien. Emily took a deep breath, marveling at the vivid hues and strange flora.

As she ventured further into this new world, she encountered creatures she had never seen before—delicate, luminescent beings that fluttered like fireflies, and plants with bioluminescent petals that pulsed gently in the twilight. The landscape was both enchanting and unsettling, a stark contrast to the fog-covered town she had left behind.

Emily walked cautiously, her senses alert to every new sound and sight. She came across a small, crystalline pond with waters that seemed to reflect not just her image but fragments of memories—flashes of scenes from her past and vague glimpses of unknown places. The pond's surface rippled with each movement, creating patterns that suggested deeper meanings.

After some time, Emily noticed a faint glow emanating from the depths of the forest. Driven by curiosity, she followed the light through the trees. It led her to a grand, ancient structure partially obscured by the foliage. The architecture was unlike anything she had seen—towering spires and arched doorways crafted from materials that seemed to shift colors in the light.

As she approached, she saw inscriptions on the walls of the structure, similar to those on the archway but more elaborate. They seemed to tell a story, a history of the realm and its

11

connection to the world Emily knew. The structure's entrance was guarded by stone statues, their eyes seeming to follow her every move.

Emily hesitated for a moment before stepping inside. The interior was a vast, open hall filled with intricate carvings and glowing symbols. At the center of the hall was a large, ornate pedestal, upon which rested an ancient tome bound in worn leather. The tome's cover was embossed with the same symbols she had seen throughout the realm.

With trembling hands, Emily reached for the tome. As she opened it, a surge of warmth spread through her, and the pages seemed to come alive with vibrant colors and shifting text. The book contained records of the realm's history, maps, and prophecies. Among the writings were references to the mist, the hidden portal, and the realm's purpose—guarding ancient knowledge and powers.

Emily's mind raced as she absorbed the information. The tome revealed that the realm was not just a hidden world but a place of great significance, crucial to the balance between worlds. The mist, it seemed, was a means of connecting these realms during moments of great need.

As she closed the tome, Emily felt a renewed sense of purpose. She had discovered the hidden portal and unlocked the gateway to a world full of secrets and mysteries. The realm held answers to the questions she had been asking, and perhaps even solutions to the challenges ahead.

With the tome in hand and her resolve strengthened, Emily prepared to delve deeper into the realm. The journey was just beginning, and she was determined to uncover the truth and fulfill whatever destiny awaited her in this extraordinary place.

4

Whispers in the Shadows

Emily Carter walked through the grand hall, her footsteps echoing softly against the polished stone floor. The tome she had discovered in the hidden realm's ancient structure was a source of both awe and trepidation. It was filled with cryptic inscriptions and ancient knowledge, but it was also heavy with the weight of responsibility and mystery. She had spent hours poring over its pages, trying to understand the significance of the prophecies and the connections between the realm and her own world.

The hall was dimly lit, with only the faint glow from the glowing symbols casting shadows that danced on the walls. The air was thick with an almost palpable sense of anticipation. Emily's senses were on high alert, every rustle and whisper in the dark corners catching her attention. It was as if the very shadows were alive, whispering secrets she could not quite decipher.

As she moved further into the hall, Emily noticed a subtle shift in the atmosphere. The whispers grew more distinct, though she could not make out the words. They seemed to come from everywhere and nowhere at once, a cacophony of voices that filled the silence with an eerie presence. She paused, her heart racing as she strained to catch any coherent sound.

A flicker of movement caught her eye. In the corner of the hall, a shadow seemed to separate from the darkness, taking on a more defined shape. Emily's breath caught in her throat as the shadow slowly took form, revealing a figure draped in a flowing cloak. The figure's face was obscured by a hood, and its presence was both captivating and menacing.

"Who's there?" Emily called out, her voice echoing through the hall.

The figure did not immediately respond but instead stepped forward, its movements fluid and graceful. The whispers grew louder, though still unintelligible. Emily's unease deepened, and she took a cautious step back, her fingers tightening around the tome she held.

"Do not be afraid," the figure's voice was soft but carried an authoritative undertone. It was neither male nor female, but something otherworldly—an echo of an age-old presence. "I am a keeper of the realm's secrets."

Emily's curiosity overcame her fear. "What are these whispers? Why do they seem so urgent?"

The figure's hooded head tilted slightly as if considering her question. "The whispers are the voices of those who once walked these halls. They are the echoes of knowledge and history, seeking to guide those who come after. But not all whispers are benevolent; some are warnings."

Emily's eyes widened. "Warnings about what?"

The figure's form seemed to waver, the shadows around it swirling with an almost sentient energy. "The mist that envelops your world is more than just a veil. It is a bridge between realms, a conduit for ancient powers that seek to return. The hidden portal you found is one of many, but it is also one of the most significant."

Emily's mind raced with the implications. "What powers are you talking about? And why are they seeking to return?"

"The powers of the old world, the forces that were once banished or sealed away," the figure explained, its voice growing more intense. "They lie dormant, waiting for a chance to break free. The realm you now inhabit is a key to their resurgence. But their return would mean chaos, a merging of worlds that could bring untold suffering."

The figure's words struck Emily with a sense of foreboding. She had hoped that uncovering the realm's secrets would provide clarity, but now she felt as if she was standing on the edge of a precipice. "How can I stop them?" she asked, her voice trembling slightly.

The figure seemed to consider her question for a moment. "To prevent their return, you must seek the Heart of the Realm. It is a place of great power, where the balance between worlds can be maintained. But beware, for it is guarded by ancient forces and hidden from those who are unprepared."

Emily felt a surge of determination. The task ahead was daunting, but she knew she had no choice but to accept it. The safety of both her world and the hidden realm depended on her ability to navigate these challenges. "Where can I find the Heart of the Realm?" she asked.

The figure raised a gloved hand, pointing toward the far end of the hall. "Follow the path of the stars. The Heart lies where the light of the heavens meets the earth of this realm. Seek the guidance of the ancient ones and heed their warnings."

With that, the figure began to dissolve into the shadows, its form fading as if it were part of the mist itself. The whispers grew fainter, leaving Emily alone once more in the dimly lit hall. The figure's words echoed in her mind, a haunting reminder of the task before her.

Determined to heed the figure's advice, Emily turned toward the direction indicated. She knew the journey to the Heart of the Realm would be fraught with peril, but it was a path she had to take. The fate of both her world and the hidden realm depended on her actions.

As she ventured deeper into the ancient structure, the whispers of the shadows seemed to guide her, offering both warnings and encouragement. Emily's resolve hardened with each step. The hidden realm was a place of mystery and danger, but she was ready to face whatever challenges lay ahead in her quest to protect both worlds from the ancient powers seeking to return.

5

The Enchanted Forest

Emily Carter stepped out of the grand hall and into the realm's vast, otherworldly landscape. The forest beyond the ancient structure was alive with vibrant colors and strange, ethereal light. Her journey toward the Heart of the Realm was about to begin, and the first part of her quest led her into the heart of the Enchanted Forest.

The forest was unlike any she had ever seen. Trees with glowing leaves towered above her, their trunks shimmering with hues of silver and gold. The ground was covered in a soft, luminescent moss that gave off a gentle, inviting glow. The air was filled with the sweet scent of unfamiliar flowers, and the faint, melodic hum of magical energy resonated through the forest, creating a symphony of nature that was both soothing and otherworldly.

Emily followed a narrow path that meandered through the forest. The path was marked by glowing sigils embedded in the trees, their soft light guiding her way. As she walked, she couldn't help but marvel at the beauty around her. The forest seemed almost sentient, responding to her presence with subtle changes in the light and the gentle rustle of leaves.

The deeper she ventured into the Enchanted Forest, the more she noticed that the forest seemed to be alive. Small, luminous creatures flitted through the air, their wings leaving trails of sparkling light. They looked like a cross between fireflies and butterflies, their delicate forms glowing with an inner radiance. Occasionally, a low, melodic chime would ring out from somewhere in the forest, adding to the magical ambiance.

Despite the beauty, there was an undercurrent of unease. The forest was not just a realm of wonder but also one of profound mystery. Shadows seemed to shift in the corners of her vision, and the deeper she went, the more she felt as though she was being watched. The whispers from the shadows in the ancient hall seemed to follow her, their voices blending with the rustling leaves and the distant, melodious chimes.

Suddenly, Emily came upon a clearing, its center dominated by a large, ancient tree. The tree was massive, its branches spreading out like an enormous canopy, and its bark was covered in intricate carvings that glowed softly in the dim light. At the base of the tree was a small, crystal-clear pool of water, its surface reflecting the light of the tree's bioluminescent leaves.

Drawn by the beauty of the scene, Emily approached the pool. As she neared, she noticed that the water was not just clear but seemed to have a depth that went beyond its physical dimensions. It appeared to be a portal to another world, or perhaps a window into the mysteries of the forest.

She leaned over the pool, and the surface began to ripple. The ripples formed into images—visions of other travelers who had ventured into the forest before her. Some of the images showed people navigating the same path she was on, while others depicted those who had lost their way. The visions were accompanied by faint whispers, which Emily could barely make out.

One image, in particular, caught her attention. It showed a figure, cloaked in shadow, standing in the midst of the forest. The figure seemed to be waiting for something, or someone, and the aura of anticipation around it was palpable. Emily's heart raced. Could this be another guardian of the forest, or perhaps an ally she would encounter on her journey?

Determined to uncover more, Emily turned away from the pool and continued along the path. As she walked, she came across various magical creatures and artifacts. Glowing flowers that sang when touched, small fae beings that offered cryptic advice, and ancient stones inscribed with runes of power were scattered throughout the forest. Each discovery seemed to guide her further, revealing more about the forest's enchantments and secrets.

Eventually, Emily arrived at a large, moss-covered archway partially concealed by vines and flowering plants. The archway was similar in style to the one she had found at the edge of the forest but was adorned with even more elaborate carvings and symbols. The archway seemed to pulse with a gentle, welcoming energy, as if it were inviting her to pass through.

With a deep breath, Emily stepped through the archway. As she did, she felt a sudden shift in the atmosphere. The forest on the other side was even more enchanting, with luminous flora that seemed to communicate with each other through light and sound. The path ahead was marked by floating lanterns that flickered softly, casting a warm, golden glow on the path.

The deeper she went, the more she felt a sense of purpose. The Enchanted Forest was guiding her toward something significant, and every step she took brought her closer to her goal. The path through the forest was filled with both wonder and challenges, but Emily was determined to press on.

As she ventured further, she encountered a series of trials designed to test her resolve and wisdom. Magical barriers that required her to solve riddles, illusions that challenged her perception, and trials of courage that forced her to confront her deepest fears. Each trial was a step toward understanding the true nature of the Enchanted Forest and her role in the unfolding events.

Emily emerged from the trials with newfound strength and clarity. The Enchanted Forest had tested her, but it had also revealed its true nature—a place of magic and mystery that held the key to unlocking the secrets of the realm. With a renewed sense of purpose, Emily continued her journey, knowing that the Heart of the Realm was still ahead, waiting to be discovered.

6

The Cursed City

As Emily Carter ventured deeper into the hidden realm, the landscape began to shift. The vibrant, living magic of the Enchanted Forest gradually gave way to a stark, unsettling terrain. The path led her out of the lush greenery and into a barren expanse, where the air was thick with a sense of desolation. The fog had returned, heavier and more oppressive, swirling in gray mists that clung to everything like a shroud.

In the distance, Emily could see the crumbling remains of what appeared to be an ancient city. The architecture was grand and elaborate, but the buildings were now in ruins, their once-majestic spires and domes reduced to skeletal frameworks. The city seemed to stretch endlessly, with streets lined by decaying structures and statues half-buried in debris. The atmosphere was thick with an eerie silence, broken only by the occasional distant echo of what might have been a long-forgotten sound.

As Emily approached the edge of the cursed city, she noticed that the mist around her grew denser, and a cold wind began to blow. The wind carried whispers that seemed to come from nowhere and everywhere at once, fragments of voices that drifted on the air like mournful echoes of the past.

The city's once-grand archways and columns were now weathered and cracked. Ivy and other creeping plants had overgrown much of the ruins, their dark tendrils twisting through the broken stone. Emily tread carefully, her footsteps cautious as she navigated through the debris-strewn streets. The oppressive gloom of the city made her feel as though she was walking through a forgotten dream, where time had come to a standstill and the past lingered like a specter.

She soon came across a large, ornate fountain in the center of what must have once been a bustling plaza. Now, the fountain was dry and choked with grime, its carved figures eroded by time. The air around it seemed to shimmer faintly with a ghostly light, and Emily felt a chill run down her spine. She could almost sense the presence of something malevolent, a lingering energy that had turned this place into a shadow of its former self.

Curiosity and resolve pushed her onward. As she explored the city, she discovered signs of an ancient and powerful curse that had befallen it. There were strange symbols etched into the walls, their meanings lost to the ages but clearly intended as warnings. In some places, Emily found remnants of old magical wards and barriers, now broken and faded. The curses and traps had once been designed to protect or imprison something, but now they were just echoes of a long-forgotten conflict.

Emily's journey led her to a grand palace at the heart of the city. The palace was the most intact structure she had seen so far, though it too showed signs of decay. The once-lustrous gold and marble were tarnished and cracked, and the vast doors were partially ajar, creaking in the wind. Emily pushed the doors open and stepped inside.

The interior of the palace was both magnificent and eerie. Elaborate tapestries and faded murals adorned the walls, depicting scenes of battles, celebrations, and what looked like the city's golden age. The grand hall was empty except for a large, dusty throne at its center. The throne was adorned with the same symbols she had seen throughout the city, and a sense of foreboding seemed to emanate from it.

Emily approached the throne, her footsteps echoing loudly in the silent hall. As she drew closer, she noticed a series of inscriptions carved into the throne's base. The inscriptions were written in an ancient script, but Emily could make out enough to understand that they spoke of a great betrayal and a curse cast upon the city by its own rulers.

The text described how the city's leaders had summoned a powerful force to protect their realm from an external threat. However, the power they summoned had become uncontrollable, leading to the city's downfall. The curse had been a desperate measure to contain the unleashed force, but it had ultimately doomed the city to eternal decay.

Emily felt a pang of sympathy for the city's lost inhabitants. The grandeur of the palace and the remnants of its former glory spoke of a civilization that had once been vibrant and prosperous, now reduced to a cautionary tale. The whispers in the wind seemed to tell stories of the city's fall, mingling with her thoughts and fueling her resolve to uncover more.

Determined to find answers, Emily searched the palace for any clues or artifacts that might shed light on how the curse could be lifted or what had caused the city's downfall. In one of the palace's side chambers, she discovered an ancient chest covered in dust and cobwebs. With a deep breath, she opened it, revealing a collection of old scrolls and a small, intricately carved box.

The scrolls were brittle and delicate, but Emily managed to unfurl them carefully. They contained detailed records of the city's history, including descriptions of the rituals and spells used in the city's final moments. The small box, when opened, revealed a collection of crystals and enchanted items that seemed to resonate with a faint, magical energy.

Emily realized that these items might hold the key to under-standing the curse and potentially finding a way to lift it. She gathered the scrolls and crystals, tucking them into her satchel. As she prepared to leave the palace, the whispers grew louder, as if urging her to hurry. The oppressive mist seemed to close in around her, and she felt a renewed urgency to continue her journey.

As Emily exited the palace and retraced her steps through the desolate city, she knew that the cursed city's secrets were not just historical curiosities but were deeply intertwined with the fate of the realm. The knowledge she had gathered might be crucial in her quest to protect both her world and the hidden realm from the ancient forces seeking to return.

With the scrolls and crystals in hand, Emily made her way back to the edge of the cursed city. The mist swirled around her as she left the ruins behind, and she could sense that her journey was far from over. The challenges ahead were unknown, but she was determined to uncover the truth and find a way to restore balance to the realm.

7

The Enigmatic Oracle

The journey from the cursed city had left Emily Carter weary but determined. As she traversed the desolate landscape, the fog lifted slightly, revealing a path that led into a more serene part of the realm. The knowledge she had gathered from the city's ruins weighed heavily on her, and the scrolls and crystals she carried seemed to hum with latent energy. The path before her promised a new chapter in her quest: the search for the enigmatic oracle.

The scrolls had hinted at the existence of an oracle, a seer who resided deep within the realm's Sacred Grove. The oracle was said to possess profound wisdom and the ability to guide those who sought to restore balance to the world. Emily hoped that this oracle could provide the guidance she needed to navigate the dangers that lay ahead.

The path through the Sacred Grove was marked by ancient,

towering trees whose branches intertwined to form a lush canopy overhead. Unlike the barren, mist-shrouded city, this forest was alive with vibrant, emerald green. The air was filled with the sweet scent of blooming flowers and the gentle murmur of a nearby stream. Sunlight filtered through the foliage, casting a dappled, golden light on the forest floor.

As Emily ventured deeper into the grove, she noticed that the trees seemed to part in response to her presence, creating a clear path that led further into the heart of the forest. It was as if the forest itself was guiding her toward the oracle. The path was lined with delicate, glowing flowers that pulsed gently, illuminating her way with a soft, calming light.

After a few hours of walking, Emily reached a clearing dominated by an ancient stone altar. The altar was covered in intricate carvings and surrounded by a circle of large, smooth stones. At the center of the clearing stood a tall, graceful figure cloaked in a robe of shimmering silver and blue. The figure's face was obscured by a hood, but Emily could feel the powerful presence of the oracle even from a distance.

As Emily approached the altar, the oracle spoke, their voice a soft, melodious tone that seemed to resonate with the very essence of the grove. "Welcome, seeker. I have been expecting you."

Emily took a deep breath, feeling a mixture of awe and nervous anticipation. "I seek guidance," she said. "The realm is in turmoil, and I need to understand how to restore balance."

The oracle extended a slender hand, beckoning Emily closer. "Come forward. The answers you seek are not always what they seem. To understand the path ahead, you must first confront the truths within yourself."

Emily stepped closer to the altar, her heart pounding. The oracle's presence was both soothing and intimidating, and she felt an almost tangible sense of magic in the air. The oracle began to speak, their voice weaving a tapestry of ancient lore and prophetic visions.

"The balance of the realms is delicate," the oracle began. "The mist that bridges worlds is a conduit for both creation and destruction. It holds the power to connect disparate realms, but it also harbors forces that can unravel the fabric of existence if not properly managed."

The oracle paused, their eyes hidden but still seeming to pierce through to Emily's very soul. "You have seen the consequences of the curse in the Cursed City. You have felt the whispers of the shadows and the guidance of the Enchanted Forest. Each of these encounters has been a test, a piece of the puzzle that you must now piece together."

Emily nodded, trying to absorb the weight of the oracle's words. "What must I do to prevent the ancient powers from breaking free and causing chaos?"

The oracle reached into the folds of their robe and produced a small, ornate box. They placed it on the altar before Emily. "Within this box lies a key to restoring balance. It is an artifact of great power, but its true nature can only be revealed through understanding and introspection."

Emily carefully opened the box, revealing a beautifully crafted crystal orb. The orb glowed with a deep, pulsating light that seemed to respond to her touch. The light within the orb shifted colors, swirling with patterns that seemed to tell a story of their own.

"This orb," the oracle explained, "is a vessel of truth and clarity. It will reveal to you the path you must take and the sacrifices you may need to make. But be warned: it will also show you the depths of your own heart and the choices that define your destiny."

Emily held the orb in her hands, feeling its warmth and the gentle hum of energy it radiated. She closed her eyes and focused, allowing herself to be open to the visions and insights that the orb might provide.

As she gazed into the orb, images began to materialize. She saw scenes of the hidden realm's past, its struggles and triumphs, the rise and fall of ancient civilizations. The visions shifted to her own world, showing the impact of the mist and the dangers it posed. The orb's light revealed potential futures, paths that could lead to salvation or destruction depending on the choices she made.

The orb also revealed a vision of herself, standing at a crossroads with two distinct paths before her. One path led to a realm of peace and harmony, while the other descended into chaos and ruin. The choice was not just about actions but also about embracing her true purpose and accepting the sacrifices required to achieve her goals.

Emily's mind was overwhelmed by the intensity of the visions. She saw the importance of her role in both worlds and the need to make difficult decisions to protect them. The oracle's guidance was becoming clearer, but it also came with the realization of the immense responsibility she bore.

When the visions faded, Emily looked up at the oracle with newfound determination. "I understand now. The path ahead is fraught with challenges, but I must follow it to restore balance and protect both worlds."

The oracle nodded, their voice calm and reassuring. "You have the wisdom and courage to face what lies ahead. Remember that the orb's light will guide you, but the choices you make will shape the outcome. Trust in yourself and the journey you are destined to undertake."

With the oracle's blessing and the orb in hand, Emily prepared to leave the Sacred Grove. She felt a renewed sense of purpose and clarity about her quest. The journey was far from over, but with the guidance of the enigmatic oracle, she was ready to face the challenges that lay ahead and work toward restoring balance to the realms.

8

The Labyrinth of Echoes

Emily Carter stepped out of the Sacred Grove, clutching the crystal orb tightly. The grove's ethereal beauty had offered her clarity, but now she faced a new and daunting challenge: the Labyrinth of Echoes. According to the oracle, the labyrinth was a place of trials, where echoes of the past and future converged, and only those who could navigate its complexities would find the path to the Heart of the Realm.

The landscape surrounding the grove had transformed. What was once a serene forest now gave way to a stark, desolate plateau. The air was heavy with a cold wind that carried faint, distant whispers. In the distance, Emily could see the entrance to the labyrinth: a towering, arching gateway made of dark, ancient stone. The entrance was partially obscured by swirling mist, and the labyrinth's shadow seemed to stretch endlessly into the horizon.

As Emily approached the gateway, she felt an uneasy chill. The labyrinth was said to be a place where one's deepest fears and desires came to life, a place where every choice mattered and every step could lead to salvation or doom. Taking a deep breath, she stepped through the archway and into the labyrinth.

Inside, the labyrinth was an intricate network of twisting corridors and high, jagged walls. The stone was cold and rough, and the passages were dimly lit by a flickering, bluish light that seemed to emanate from the very walls themselves. The air was filled with the sounds of distant murmurs and echoes, which seemed to follow her every movement, creating an unsettling atmosphere.

Emily took out the crystal orb, which glowed softly, casting a warm light that pushed back the surrounding gloom. The orb's light illuminated the walls, revealing faint markings and symbols that seemed to shift and change as she moved. The labyrinth was a living entity, its paths constantly shifting and rearranging themselves, making navigation a challenge.

As she progressed deeper into the maze, Emily encountered various trials designed to test her resolve and intellect. The first trial came in the form of a series of puzzles. She faced a large stone door with intricate carvings and a riddle inscribed above it. The riddle spoke of time and balance, and Emily had to decipher its meaning to proceed.

After several moments of intense concentration, Emily solved the riddle. The carvings on the door shifted, revealing a hidden mechanism that allowed her to pass through. The door creaked open, and she continued on her way, more determined than ever.

The second trial was more personal. As Emily turned a corner, she was confronted with illusions of her past—images of her family, friends, and pivotal moments in her life. These illusions spoke to her, invoking both comfort and regret, and tried to sway her from her path. Emily struggled to maintain her focus, recognizing that these were merely echoes designed to distract her. She took a deep breath and pressed forward, pushing through the emotional turmoil.

Further into the labyrinth, Emily encountered a chamber filled with mirrors. Each mirror reflected not only her physical appearance but also different versions of herself, each embodying various aspects of her personality and potential futures. The mirrors spoke, offering her advice, warnings, and temptations. Emily had to discern which reflections were true and which were misleading, a challenge that required her to confront her own insecurities and desires.

The final trial of the labyrinth was a test of courage. Emily found herself in a vast, dark chamber with a deep chasm running through its center. On the other side of the chasm was another exit, and a narrow, shaky bridge spanned the gap. The whispers and echoes in the chamber grew louder, filling her with doubt and fear. Emily knew that crossing the bridge was essential, but the chasm seemed to symbolize the daunting challenges ahead.

Summoning her courage, Emily took a tentative step onto the bridge. The planks creaked and swayed under her weight, and the chasm below seemed to grow darker and deeper. With each step, the whispers became more intense, but Emily focused on the light of the crystal orb, which guided her through the darkness.

Reaching the other side, Emily found herself in a final chamber, bathed in a soft, golden light. In the center of the chamber was a pedestal, and upon it rested a large, ancient book. The book was bound in weathered leather and adorned with symbols similar to those she had encountered throughout the labyrinth.

Approaching the pedestal, Emily opened the book, revealing pages filled with ancient texts and illustrations. The book contained valuable information about the Heart of the Realm, including maps, rituals, and insights into the ancient powers that sought to return. The book also included instructions on how to use the orb she carried, detailing how to channel its energy to reveal the location of the Heart.

With the book in hand, Emily felt a renewed sense of purpose. The labyrinth had tested her resolve, but she had persevered and gained valuable knowledge. The echoes of the labyrinth were now behind her, and she was one step closer to finding the Heart of the Realm and fulfilling her mission.

As Emily exited the labyrinth, the mists cleared, revealing a new path that led toward a distant mountain range. She knew that the journey was far from over, but with the knowledge she had gained and the strength she had discovered within herself, she was ready to face whatever lay ahead. The Labyrinth of Echoes had been a significant trial, but it had also prepared her for the challenges to come.

9

The Veiled Summit

Emerging from the Labyrinth of Echoes, Emily Carter found herself at the base of a towering mountain range. The peaks loomed high above her, their snow-capped summits piercing the sky like jagged teeth. The weather was harsh and the wind howled relentlessly, but Emily's resolve was unwavering. According to the ancient book she had discovered, the Heart of the Realm was located at the summit of this treacherous range.

The path ahead was steep and challenging. The mountain paths were narrow and winding, and the cold air stung Emily's face with every step. She wrapped herself tightly in her cloak and adjusted her gear, knowing that the journey up the mountain would test her endurance and strength.

As Emily began her ascent, the landscape shifted dramatically. The lush greenery of the valley below was replaced by barren rock and ice. The snow on the ground was pristine and untouched, save for her own footprints. The mountain's beauty was stark and harsh, but there was a majesty to it that inspired awe and respect.

The higher she climbed, the more the weather intensified. A blizzard swept in, reducing visibility to mere feet. Emily pressed on, guided by the map in the ancient book and the glowing crystal orb that seemed to pulse with a steady rhythm. The orb's light cut through the swirling snow, creating a narrow beacon in the whiteout conditions.

As she climbed, Emily encountered several hazards. Icy ledges and treacherous slopes required careful navigation, and sudden avalanches posed a constant threat. The cold was biting and relentless, sapping her energy with every gust of wind. But her determination kept her moving forward, step by painstaking step.

Hours turned into days as she climbed higher. The mountain's harsh environment was unforgiving, and Emily's progress was slow. At night, she found shelter in small caves and crevices, huddling for warmth and rest. Each day, she woke to the same harsh conditions, but the thought of reaching the summit drove her forward.

On the third day, as the blizzard subsided, Emily came across an ancient structure partially buried in snow and ice. It appeared to be a temple or an observatory, its stone walls weathered but still standing. Intrigued, Emily approached the structure, hoping it might provide clues or respite from the harsh conditions.

The entrance to the structure was partially blocked by snow, but Emily managed to clear a path. Inside, she found a vast chamber adorned with ancient tapestries and murals. The walls were covered in inscriptions and celestial maps, depicting the alignment of stars and constellations. The structure seemed to be a place of great significance, possibly used for observing the heavens or performing ancient rituals.

In the center of the chamber stood a pedestal, upon which rested a large, intricately carved crystal. The crystal was similar in design to the orb Emily carried but was much larger and seemed to glow with an inner light. The inscriptions on the walls hinted that this crystal was a key to unlocking the final path to the summit.

Emily carefully examined the crystal and the surrounding inscriptions. She deciphered that the crystal needed to be aligned with the constellations depicted on the walls to reveal the final path to the summit. Using the knowledge she had gained from the ancient book and her observations of the stars, she positioned the crystal according to the celestial alignments.

As she completed the alignment, the crystal began to shine brightly, and the walls of the chamber shifted, revealing a hidden passage. The passage was narrow but led upward, and Emily could see a faint, shimmering light at its end. With renewed hope and determination, she ventured into the passage.

The final stretch of the climb was both exhilarating and exhausting. The passage led to a small plateau near the summit, where the wind howled fiercely and the air was thin. The view from the plateau was breathtaking, offering a panoramic vista of the entire realm. Emily could see the vast landscapes she had traversed and the distant horizon beyond.

At the center of the plateau stood an ancient altar, covered in frost and snow. The altar was adorned with intricate carvings and symbols that matched those in the ancient book. Emily approached the altar, feeling a sense of reverence and anticipation. She placed the crystal orb on the altar, and as she did, the symbols began to glow with a warm, golden light.

The light from the altar grew brighter, and a hidden chamber beneath the plateau began to reveal itself. Emily descended into the chamber, where she found a magnificent chamber illuminated by a radiant, ethereal light. In the center of the chamber was a large, pulsating crystal, the Heart of the Realm.

The Heart of the Realm was a stunning sight—a massive, crystalline structure that seemed to capture and reflect the essence of all the magic and power within the realm. Its light bathed the chamber in a warm, soothing glow, and Emily could feel its energy resonating with the crystal orb she carried.

As she approached the Heart, the orb began to pulse in harmony with the crystal, and the chamber filled with a sense of profound peace and unity. Emily knew that she had reached the culmination of her journey. The Heart of the Realm represented the balance and harmony she had sought to restore, and its presence signified the beginning of a new chapter for the realm.

Emily reached out and touched the Heart of the Realm, and as she did, she felt a surge of energy flow through her. The crystal's power enveloped her, and she could sense the ancient magic being reawakened. The realm's balance was being restored, and the forces that had threatened it were being brought into harmony.

With a deep sense of fulfillment and a renewed commitment to her mission, Emily knew that her journey was not yet complete. The Heart of the Realm had been restored, but there were still challenges ahead. She had to ensure that the balance was maintained and that the realm would thrive in the days to come.

As she prepared to leave the summit and return to her world, Emily felt a deep sense of accomplishment. The Veiled Summit had tested her resolve and strength, but it had also revealed the true power and beauty of the realm. With the Heart of the Realm now secure, she was ready to face whatever challenges lay ahead and to continue her quest to protect and restore balance to both worlds.

10

The Shattered Convergence

Descending from the Veiled Summit, Emily Carter felt a pro-found sense of accomplishment and a renewed purpose. The Heart of the Realm was now secure, its power restored, and the realm's balance was beginning to stabilize. But her journey was not yet complete. The ancient book she had found in the Labyrinth of Echoes had hinted at a final convergence— a moment when all the forces she had encountered would come together, revealing the true scope of the threat and the ultimate challenge she would face.

The descent was as treacherous as the ascent, but Emily moved with a determined pace. She navigated the icy slopes with practiced skill, guided by the light of the crystal orb, which still pulsed warmly in her hands. The realm had begun to change subtly; the oppressive mists that once obscured the land were clearing, revealing glimpses of a world in transition.

Returning to the valley below, Emily noticed a gathering of storm clouds on the horizon. The sky was darkening, and the air crackled with a sense of impending storm. The convergence was approaching, and she needed to act quickly. The ancient book had mentioned that the final convergence would be marked by a great tempest, a clash of energies that would determine the fate of both worlds.

Her first task was to return to the Enchanted Forest. The forest had been a place of guidance and refuge, and she hoped that its magic might offer further insight into the coming convergence. The journey through the forest was marked by an eerie calm; the usual symphony of magical creatures and rustling leaves was subdued, as if the forest itself was holding its breath.

Upon reaching the heart of the forest, Emily found the grove where she had first met the oracle. The once-vibrant area was now filled with an unsettling stillness. The trees stood silent, their branches heavy with anticipation. She approached the central clearing, where the oracle's presence was palpable, though the oracle themselves was nowhere to be seen.

Emily set up camp in the grove and began to study the ancient book and the Heart of the Realm's crystal orb. The book detailed rituals and spells meant to channel and harmonize the energies of the realm. She read through the instructions carefully, realizing that she would need to perform a ritual at the convergence point to stabilize the realm and ensure its safety.

The book mentioned that the convergence would occur at a specific location known as the Nexus of Worlds, a place where the boundaries between different realms were thin. The Nexus was said to be a location of immense power, and it was here that the final ritual would be performed.

With the knowledge she had gathered, Emily set out towards the Nexus of Worlds. The journey took her through diverse landscapes—rolling hills, winding rivers, and desolate plains— each area marked by subtle signs of the realm's unrest. The once-clear sky was now filled with swirling clouds, and the air was charged with magical energy.

As she neared the Nexus, the ground began to tremble, and the sky darkened further. Emily felt a powerful surge of energy, as if the very fabric of reality was being stretched and strained. The Nexus of Worlds was a massive, ancient stone structure, partially buried in the earth and covered with intricate runes and symbols. The structure appeared to be a convergence point of ley lines, magical energy channels that crisscrossed the realm.

The storm that had been brewing finally broke, unleashing a tempest of wind, lightning, and rain. The energy at the Nexus was palpable, crackling with raw power. Emily could see the energy lines converging and intertwining, creating a web of light and shadow. The convergence was a chaotic and awe-inspiring sight, and she knew that she had to act quickly to harness and stabilize the energies.

Emily approached the Nexus and began to set up the ritual as described in the ancient book. She positioned the Heart of the Realm's crystal orb at the center of the Nexus, aligning it with the ley lines and the symbols carved into the stones. She began the incantations, her voice steady despite the raging storm around her.

The ritual involved channeling the energy from the crystal orb into the Nexus, harmonizing it with the ley lines and the ambient magical forces. Emily could feel the immense power surging through her, and she concentrated on maintaining focus and balance. The convergence was creating powerful fluctuations in the energy, and she had to keep the ritual steady to prevent a catastrophic failure.

The storm intensified as Emily continued the ritual, lightning striking the Nexus and causing the stones to glow with an otherworldly light. The energy of the Heart of the Realm pulsed in harmony with the ley lines, creating a brilliant display of interconnected magic. Emily felt a profound connection to the realm, and she realized that she was not just restoring balance but also binding the energies of the different worlds together.

As the ritual reached its climax, the storm began to subside, and the energy at the Nexus stabilized. The tumultuous energy lines settled into a harmonious pattern, and the sky began to clear. The tempest that had threatened to tear the realms apart was now dissipating, replaced by a calm, serene atmosphere.

Exhausted but triumphant, Emily completed the final incantations and sealed the ritual. The Nexus of Worlds had been stabilized, and the convergence had been successfully managed. The realm's balance was restored, and the powerful energies had been harmonized.

With the storm cleared and the Nexus stabilized, Emily took a moment to reflect on her journey. She had faced numerous challenges, uncovered ancient secrets, and restored the Heart of the Realm. Her efforts had averted a great catastrophe and ensured the safety of both worlds.

As she prepared to leave the Nexus and return to her world, Emily felt a deep sense of fulfillment. The journey had been arduous and fraught with danger, but it had also been a profound learning experience. She had grown stronger, wiser, and more connected to the magical forces of the realm.

The final convergence had tested her abilities and resolve, but it had also shown her the true power of unity and balance. With the realms now secure, Emily knew that she had played a vital role in preserving their harmony. The adventure had come to a close, but the lessons learned and the connections forged would stay with her forever.

11

The Awakening Storm

Emily Carter's return from the Nexus of Worlds marked a moment of both relief and trepidation. The storm had passed, leaving behind a transformed realm, but the journey was not yet complete. The realm had begun to heal, but disturbances were still rippling through the fabric of reality. A new challenge loomed on the horizon: the Awakening Storm, an unforeseen consequence of the convergence that threatened to undo the delicate balance she had fought so hard to achieve.

As Emily made her way back to the now-clearing landscape, she noticed subtle changes in the environment. The once-ominous mists had begun to recede, revealing vibrant patches of flora and new life. Yet, despite these signs of recovery, there was an unsettling energy in the air. The tranquil beauty of the realm was overshadowed by a lingering tension.

The path to her next destination was unclear, but the ancient book she had carried through the labyrinth contained cryptic references to the Awakening Storm. According to the book, the storm was a manifestation of residual, chaotic energy that had been stirred up during the convergence. It was a storm not of wind and rain, but of elemental and magical forces that could destabilize the realm if left unchecked.

Emily's first objective was to investigate the disturbances reported by the local inhabitants. She made her way to a nearby village that had previously been affected by the cursed mists. The village, known as Eldergrove, was now a place of uncertainty and apprehension. The villagers spoke of strange phenomena: unseasonal weather, erratic magical surges, and mysterious disappearances.

Upon arrival, Emily was greeted by the village elder, a wise woman named Liora. Liora had been a guiding force for her people during the turmoil, and she welcomed Emily with a mixture of relief and concern.

"Emily, it's good to see you," Liora said, her eyes filled with a deep, knowing sadness. "We've been facing strange occurrences since the storm cleared. It seems the balance you worked so hard to restore is still in peril."

Emily nodded, understanding the gravity of the situation. "I've seen signs of the Awakening Storm, and I need to understand more about these disturbances. What exactly have you been experiencing?"

Liora led Emily to a central meeting hall where villagers gathered to discuss their concerns. As they spoke, Emily learned about the peculiar events: sudden gusts of wind that caused havoc, unexplained bursts of magic that disrupted daily life, and a growing sense of unease among the people. The villagers described a pattern of these disturbances that hinted at an underlying cause.

The elder shared that a group of scholars and mages had been investigating the phenomena, and they believed that the Awakening Storm might be linked to an ancient artifact—the Tempest Stone. The Tempest Stone was said to be a powerful relic capable of controlling elemental forces, and it was rumored to have been hidden away centuries ago to prevent its misuse.

Emily decided that locating the Tempest Stone would be crucial to addressing the ongoing disturbances. She consulted the ancient book and discovered that the Tempest Stone was likely hidden in a place called the Stormspire, a remote, ancient tower said to be lost in the wilderness.

Guided by the information from the book and the descriptions from the villagers, Emily embarked on a quest to find the Stormspire. The journey took her through rugged terrain and dense forests, and she faced numerous obstacles along the way. The residual effects of the Awakening Storm made the journey more perilous, with sudden bursts of wind and erratic magical surges posing constant threats.

After several days of arduous travel, Emily arrived at the Storm-spire, a towering structure partially obscured by mist and encased in a protective barrier. The tower was ancient and weathered, its stones etched with elemental symbols and runes. The Tempest Stone was rumored to be hidden within the tower, but accessing it would require overcoming a series of trials designed to test one's control over elemental forces.

The entrance to the Stormspire was guarded by a series of elemental challenges. Emily had to navigate through a labyrinth of fire, ice, wind, and earth, each challenge testing her ability to harness and balance the elemental forces. The trials were both physically and mentally demanding, and Emily had to use her knowledge of magic and her innate strength to overcome them.

The trial of fire involved crossing a raging inferno, where Emily had to use her wits and magical abilities to create a protective barrier. The ice trial required her to navigate a frozen maze while avoiding dangerous ice formations and blizzards. The wind trial tested her agility and control over gusts and whirlwinds, while the earth trial challenged her to move through shifting rock and debris.

Each trial was a test of Emily's resolve and resourcefulness. She faced her fears and doubts head-on, drawing on the knowledge she had gained throughout her journey. The elemental challenges were not just physical obstacles but also symbolic of the internal struggles she had endured.

After successfully completing the trials, Emily reached the inner sanctum of the Stormspire, where the Tempest Stone was kept. The stone was an impressive relic, a crystal embedded with swirling, multicolored energy that pulsed with immense power. The Tempest Stone was both beautiful and ominous, its presence a reminder of the raw, untamed forces it could command.

Emily carefully approached the stone, knowing that activating it would require precise control and understanding of the elemental forces. Using the knowledge from the ancient book, she performed a ritual to stabilize the Tempest Stone and integrate it with the realm's energy. The ritual involved aligning the stone with the ley lines and channeling the elemental forces into a harmonious state.

As Emily completed the ritual, the Tempest Stone's energy began to stabilize, and the chaotic disturbances in the realm started to diminish. The wind settled, the magical surges became less erratic, and a sense of calm returned to the environment. The balance that Emily had worked so hard to restore was being reinforced by the Tempest Stone.

With the Tempest Stone secured and its power harmonized, Emily prepared to return to Eldergrove. She knew that her actions had addressed the immediate threat of the Awakening Storm, but there was still work to be done to ensure the realm's long-term stability.

Upon her return, the villagers greeted her with gratitude and relief. The disturbances had lessened, and a sense of normalcy was beginning to return. Emily shared her findings and the successful stabilization of the Tempest Stone, providing hope for a brighter future.

As the realm began to heal and recover from the Awakening Storm, Emily reflected on her journey. She had faced numerous challenges and uncovered deep truths about the nature of balance and harmony. The trials had tested her strength and resolve, but they had also deepened her understanding of the magical forces that shaped the world.

With the Tempest Stone secured and the realm's balance restored, Emily knew that her quest was nearing its end. The challenges she had faced had prepared her for the final steps of her journey, and she was ready to face whatever lay ahead with a renewed sense of purpose and determination.

12

The Legacy of Harmony

Emily Carter stood at the edge of Eldergrove, the village that had been her sanctuary during the trials of the Awakening Storm. The realm was visibly transformed, its balance restored and its elemental forces harmonized. The skies were clear, the landscapes vibrant, and the people of Eldergrove were once again filled with hope and gratitude. Yet, Emily knew that her journey was nearing its end, and it was time to address the final challenge: ensuring the realm's future and leaving behind a legacy of harmony.

In the days following the stabilization of the Tempest Stone, Emily had worked closely with the villagers and local scholars to consolidate her findings and reinforce the realm's newly restored balance. She had shared her knowledge of the elemental forces and the significance of the Heart of the Realm and the Tempest Stone. Her efforts had led to the establishment of new practices and rituals to maintain equilibrium and safeguard the realm from future disturbances.

One evening, as the sun set over Eldergrove, casting a warm golden light over the village, Emily gathered with Liora and the village leaders at a central meeting place. They were preparing to hold a ceremony to celebrate the restoration of balance and to honor the contributions of all those who had supported her journey.

The ceremony was held in a large clearing at the heart of Eldergrove. The area was adorned with banners and decorations symbolizing the elements and the magical forces that had been restored. The villagers gathered, their faces lit with anticipation and respect. The ceremony was not only a celebration but also a formal acknowledgment of the new practices that would help preserve the realm's harmony.

Liora addressed the crowd, her voice carrying both reverence and pride. "Today, we gather to celebrate not only the restoration of our realm but also the unity and strength that have brought us here. Emily Carter has undertaken a great journey, facing trials and overcoming challenges to restore balance and harmony to our world. Her bravery and wisdom have ensured that we can continue to thrive in peace."

Emily stepped forward, her heart swelling with gratitude. She had come a long way from the initial uncertainty and fear that had marked her journey. The realm's recovery and the villagers' support had been a testament to the strength of their collective effort and the power of harmony.

"Thank you all for your support and belief in this journey," Emily said, her voice steady despite the emotions she felt. "The challenges we faced were not mine alone to bear; they were a reflection of our collective resolve. The balance we have restored is a legacy that belongs to each of us. It is our duty to uphold and protect it."

The ceremony continued with rituals and blessings to solidify the realm's newfound stability. The villagers performed dances and songs that honored the elemental forces and the natural world. They also established new traditions and practices designed to maintain the harmony that Emily had fought to achieve.

As the ceremony drew to a close, Emily felt a deep sense of accomplishment and contentment. The legacy of her journey was not just in the actions she had taken but in the enduring changes that would benefit the realm for generations to come. The Heart of the Realm and the Tempest Stone were now safeguarded, and the knowledge she had shared would continue to guide the people of Eldergrove and beyond.

With the ceremony complete, Emily took one last walk through the village. The sky was clear, and the air was filled with the sounds of joyful celebration. She visited the places that had been significant to her journey, reflecting on the friendships she had formed and the lessons she had learned.

The time had come for Emily to leave Eldergrove and return to her own world. She knew that her departure marked the end of one chapter and the beginning of another. The realm's balance was secure, but the experiences she had gained would shape her future endeavors.

As she prepared to leave, Liora approached her with a parting gift—a beautifully crafted pendant imbued with the elemental symbols and the essence of the realm's magic. "This is a token of our gratitude and a reminder of the harmony you have helped restore. Wear it with honor, knowing that you have made a lasting impact on our world."

Emily accepted the pendant with a deep sense of appreciation. It was a symbol of the bond between her world and the realm she had helped save. With the pendant around her neck, she felt a renewed connection to the magical forces and the people who had supported her journey.

As she walked away from Eldergrove and toward the horizon, Emily looked back one last time. The village was bathed in the warm glow of twilight, a testament to the new era of peace and balance that had been achieved. She carried with her the legacy of harmony and the knowledge that she had made a difference.

Emily's journey had come full circle, from the uncertainty of her first steps to the profound understanding of balance and unity she now possessed. The realm was a place of renewed hope and promise, and she was confident that it would continue to flourish under the guardianship of its people.

With a final, resolute glance toward the realm she had saved, Emily stepped forward, ready to face the next chapter of her life with the wisdom and strength she had gained. The legacy of harmony would guide her future endeavors, and the lessons learned would remain a beacon of light in her heart.

9 787175 003401